I Knew I Was a Girl

A MEMOIR IN POETRY

Christine Quarnström

CENTRAL PARK SOUTH PUBLISHING

Publisher: Central Park South Publishing
website: www.langtonsinternational.com

Book Layout – alienartifacts

I Knew I Was a Girl by Christine Quarnström. -- 1st ed.

ISBN 978-1-7352964-2-5

For Lee,

my love, my muse

CONTENTS

1: I KNEW I WAS A GIRL

Winter Pulls Down its Shade

Winter pulls down its shade early,
gentian haze shrouding
distant hills.
The sun is a raw egg
sliding down
the throat of day.
      Unseasonably hot, I crave
the frozen storms of Midwest winters,
the ancient elms that arched over our brick street
their branches majestic in a drape of fresh snow,
skating on homemade backyard ponds
'til day closes its door at 4 o'clock.
      Night we trudged through fresh powder
runners of my brother's Red Racer digging in
under the sled's belly, the dead weight of my
bundled body as he dragged me along.
We'd glide into and out of pods of lamplight, shadows
making us taller, older somehow as we soaked up

the silence of winter.

The Empty Box They Bury

Double doors
painted daze white
cathedral high holy doors
unholy to enter.
      I wake
      lying cool as a coin
      head up
      morning moving in
      through open shutters
      light through the prism lamp
      colors unlocked -
      Windsor rose walls
      peach, mauve.
Around the corner
      one step up to
another room where
my father stands with roses;
He never brought her flowers.
Why me, now, before coffee
his blood-spattered clothes the bleach
of years couldn't
sop up?
I see him naked now
after shaving
after the ritual of shower
my dad in rib tickle corny jokes
      how men look stark naked
in the morning, his whistle down the hall
      "Hiya, I'm home!"
arms around my mother
kissing.

And now the color rose
rearranges itself
the way blue rearranged my life
the day he died.
How the walls and I wailed
wanting to keep him any way I could
taking him out of that clam-gray
satin-lined box
because he's cold,
slipping him under my royal
blue robe of denial.

I scoff at those who bury empty boxes,
heap flowers on stone cold heads.
My dad with silly roses.
mourning him
as he breaks open my day.

Freeway

Before he made up my mind
before my hot chili sex
was laid
open
     peeled
         & deveined
the seeds left in,
I was Free –
Of Mother
of her constraints
Free to mount his Triumph,
(the bike he owned with another kid & lied
about to his parents)
as I climbed aboard, a shiver of space
between two pounding breasts and
the black tundra of his leather jacket
borrowed boots kicking free from a brace of wind
kid-glove-soft that whipped past my cheeks,
as we street-biked over a web of freeways
to the beach.
California winters were wet then
as he took me home that first time in his
moon-equipped yellow-green car, the '54
Chevy with a hole in the floor
a blur of my future swirling by beneath my feet
as we spun out, hydroplaning out of control in
deep-puddle water, too much too fast
landing backwards on the outer rim
of the wet road.
        After we did *it* (his parents were down the hall)
tucked in with guilt, I felt anything but
free as he whispered,
"This is what we both wanted,
isn't it?"

The Burn

In the 40's no one seemed to care
what came after fire; we played with it, smoked,
people lit up in a romantic gesture, tip to tip
and nobody asked for the stars
when they could have the moon.
Smokes were suave -
Lucky Strike, Chesterfield, Camel,
nothing bad filtered out.
Tobacco was a dirty weed,
and we liked it.
       Growing up near Lake Michigan, leaves
came down as storm windows went up.
Giant elm and oak trees arched over cobbled streets,
their gnarled limbs frozen in a timely dance
of gold turning to sack brown.
We'd rake up mounds of brittle bodies, hurl ourselves
with death-defying leaps into massive waist-high
piles flailing arms and legs at the center of the crater,
shrieking with delight when we torched the stack,
then erupting into spasms of laughter
as we walked away. We'd leave the remains
to smolder on the blackened street.

Snapshot

Finally, she's mine
if only for one sixtieth of a second
                a smile seldom seen in pictures;
it wasn't her style.
She gazes at me, the second child,
as I perch on her knee, mouth breaking open
to expose a pink underbelly of emotion
curled up to just under the nostrils to reveal
a full arch of teeth, bleached white in the moment
of having a daughter.
            We are in the vortex of split seconds
            swirling down to mother and daughter only
but my brother is on the run to reclaim her
his right arm and left knee in motion
            eyes spearing me
            and Daddy, oblivious
his long slender fingers lined up like sentinels
on his friend's daughter's left arm
bone-white business shirt and wide tie
his eyes squinting behind glasses
into the Brownie.
For one unguarded moment,
Mother is all mine.

Me and James Dean

Ciro's on the Sunset Strip, July, 1955:

"Mental Health Benefit for Children"
No cloud-cover that night. All the stars were out:
Jack Benny, Rhonda Fleming, trailing her comet of flame-red
hair. Danny Thomas, Debbie Reynolds in pre-wedding swirls of
meringue-white gown, newly engaged to Eddie Fisher.
The day's blistering heat was still rising
off the Strip.
   At fifteen I was a fish out of water,
plucked from the Roosevelt Hotel pool, fragile after my
father's sudden death, gawky with stick-straight body, hair like
a Monet wheat stack at sunset corralled into a ponytail.
   How I hated wearing those dorky glasses and suddenly there
He was in method actor slouch, teen dream hero who, of all things,
was wearing red-rimmed glasses decked out in sartorial splendor tux,
nothing he ever wore in those iconic movies as he writhed in anguish
to defy his staid, boring parents in *Rebel Without a Cause*,
something we all wanted to do ourselves.
    Only two feet away, I clutched the camera case to my
fluttering breast as my brother snapped
me and James Dean, young and alive
for all time, the risk-taker and the romantic.

Highway 46: two months later.

Smashed like a bug on that stretch
of lone star road, dead in his
material-boy Porsche.
Gone at 24.

I knew I was a Girl

As early as five, I knew I was a girl
eyes trained on the sailor boy upstairs,
just returned from war, inert as the planked dead on
his single bed, one long arm a dangling oar that grazed
the oak floor as he slipped into the watery depths of
exhausted sleep.
  Finally home, at last his Blue Star mother could take
down the flag, clear the victory garden of its mangled roots
plant flowers instead. Yes, that day I felt it down to my little
brown oxfords, knew to the tips of slender kid fingers
that sometimes brought me curious pleasure
that I was a girl, and, one day, I imagined,
he would come for me.

Lux

As I click open the bathroom door, thick fortress wall, I think about the thin-paneled one years ago, upstairs, the one with a tiny peephole just to keep an eye on my growing up. Now I think who would care, who would look, as I unwrap the secret, Lux, short for luxury I guess, and then the smell hits me like a ton of white, perfumed brick. I continue to ceremoniously unwrap this gem as the pungency swells each nostril, flaring and wide like a horse's flank. "It's magic," I muse, picked for its fragrance, simplicity, different from all the rest of those garish bars that screamed, "Buy me!" from the supermarket shelf. Mother never picked this for me to taste on days when I was mouthy.

Carefully, I peel back the layers like so much dead skin, back to Grandma's all white bath, clean to the bone, sparkly as zoomed teeth. White on white, soft-spoken and shy like her.

I draw comfort up the silvery throat of pipe, melt into the hot steamy water, as it fogs the mirror in one final death drape. I descend one limb at a time, first a toe and then each calf until all of me is submerged. The soap flops like a wet seal between my clutching palms, slips between my thighs, playful and neat. Even the ridges of my palms are gone; I'm anonymous, disappeared, along with the cares of the day.

Lilacs

When I was a green stick of a girl
leaving lilacs behind would not be a problem.
I would never miss the need for bitter chill
the ovate leaves shaped like a heart
notched at the tenuous point of attachment.
The cones bloom, heads bowed down
from too much drink, the running of the ants
in deep fragrant purple, redder than heliotrope,
paler than an amethyst purple
winter morn.
     Years later out west,
I miss the startle of spring after a bare bones winter,
the green curtain going up one morning after opening night.
A lilac-bordered yard, the cones of blossoms purple
and white like virginal girls sashaying in the breeze above
leafy underskirts, the prick of bees to gather honey
bruised brown lips wilted after a driving rain.

I am Lina

Paulina Cristina Paulson
(in Sweden, Paulsdotter)

Lina

I am Swedish.
Jus a little bit of Sweden
in the new country.

I am gud wife.

One girl   two boys
They talk American
(We keep Swedish to ourselves).

Still
A gud silsalot
Taught white-meat-apple-herring
salad, pickled fish
from Yonson's market
on Chicago's
near North Side.

The "El" clickety clack
not one thought of
going back to visit
Bents-gaard-Hult
A town that spawned me
where we bought fish
on daily docks
and the old stinkpot father
beat the ten of us
whether we needed it or not
jus to make him feel important.

Ya,
we deserve it here
Vasa dinners var so gud
Sunday jelly-on-the-belly lutefisk
hardtack with cheese
kanuckabrød and darkly-sweet
tangy orange, Lina's limpa limpa bröd.

Ya
Var sa I was
not so gud wife
not loving him enough
told them "pray for pa"
my street car conductor, August
pa, husband who lost both legs,
says a man's
not a man who can't
put two legs under his own
kitchen table.

August, who lost his lim-
pa, lost both legs to
sugar diabetes
dead now from stubborn,
gimmicks tried that
didn't work.

I am Lina.
Old now.
Some say 80
var sa gud.

I sit.
The boy, Henning, had a boy
then a girl they named after me
Cristina, middle me.

I sit
watching candles dripping down
my sweet birthday cake.
White hair, white snow piled up
on fence post sit while a fire crackles,
poker-stirred but dying in its
cradle of iron.

Cryonics

Easter Monday,
1955:

Dad skips lunch with me
to dine with Jesus.
Risen again, he
takes Dad,

so fuck the brown gardenia
the jaundiced, fake flower hat
my mush sandwiches that wait
for his blood-spattered, rumpled
fiftyish suit. The one my Mom
drags home
in a bag.

He's dead,

word heavier than lids
swollen from crying.
My mother wears navy
to the funeral
(he hated her
in black).

I weep enough to
float stiff bodies out
of dark holes,

Jesus who has my dad,
who dries my girl's face
and makes reservations
for lunch in
His name.

Best Friend

When I learned of her mother's death at 93
secretly, I was glad, my brother feeding me the obit
into the phone from Chicago.
"At last!" I said to myself, thinking about that flamethrower's
nimbus of red hair losing all its power to bleached out old age
carrot top woman who grew the round-shouldered
daughter who curled my toes the day she showed up
and stole my best friend.
    One of the only times I can remember Mother
standing up for me, her lioness claws digging
into that dirt, cinnamon eyes glowing, burning holes
into that witch of a mother's green eye when, she sniffed,
"It's like water off a duck's back"
that *my* best friend preferred *her* daughter,
that one plus one did not make *three*
and I didn't fit in because, after all,
I wasn't "their type."
        Amazing how a 13-year-old can drown
so quickly in a scant amount of water
dripping off the back
of a duck.

Apple

I am the apple of her seed-black
mother's eye
pie-baker of memorable crust
who planted me
her taut white flesh,
brown spots of age-bruised
skin eighty,
a lady of good cook
upbringing.

When not quite pie tender, I
slipped away to marry and
transplant out West.

Had she cut the apple
differently,
a star,
all points aimed at the core
her sharp-tongued device
twisted once or twice more
to keep future seeds in
place.

There, there a
pie to feed
old age
      as my brother
Johnny stayed home to
plant,
      cook, fasten on
the land the
seed that
took root.

2: MINE

When the A-Bomb Dropped

(for Lee, 1998)

When the A-bomb dropped on
your toe creating that mushroom-shaped cloud
we were so new, like two young lovers running through
the streets of Nagasaki searching for a place to defy doom.
Finding ourselves in the bookstore, we looked up all
the info we could on diabetes, and how well I
remember your eyes locked in iron resignation saying,
really giving me permission to escape,
back to the land of single living,
if I wanted to.
But here we are seven years later,
six as citizens of the same country: home, bed, table, two
dogs, and my children to love, but the flowers keep blooming
in the rock garden of your gnarled toes, a thick crust
forming with the free flowing rivers of good
blood circulating underneath.
I know they think they can get us,
but they can't.
Even after they warned me you weren't good for
the long haul, we still stand firm on your wobbly, not-so-steady legs.
They don't know what smolders beneath the layers where you and I
were formed, the resilience, the common core
the place where we carried each other
until we met.

Wedding

(for Tony)

Vestibule,
the glass cage stutters open.
Six hundred eyes tear to
stand up flows of Handel's
water music.

Grand Wedding March

The stainless bridebird struts out
in blanc de blanc peau de soie
proud feather puffs of hair
lilybells that spangle her veiled honey face,
jiggle walk to happiness

and the altared life

over sheets of meringue
spread like flowing lava

to pink cummer-bunded groomsmen
who open the lace fan of
bridesmaids unpleated at the altar.

The blond bridegroom tassels milky white
Young as summer corn, he sways in his
plastic shoes
vows cooed
the kiss detonating
52-ranks of organ salute
explosion of flashbulbs
helping everyone see double.

At the gold-domed reception
toasts slosh over the last edges of day
ring of rock band thump-beating
with dancers up dancing.

Night crashes the party
cuts cake-feeding light, focus on
love birds blurred, their lips pecking.
Arms are hooked, sipping one another.
A single candle blown out,
with two left burning.

Valentine

(for Lee, 1999)

My Valentine's
hair spikes in the wind
grey with stalks of old newspaper
blonde. His eyes are Caribbean blue,
I could walk for miles in their shallow depths.
They well up listening to La Boheme,
making him think of me, how once when we
made love, he looked in the mirror of my face
to see himself come.
   Time to part, we stand close as tree trunks.
 He branches over and we adjust the fit, wedge
in together, then lumber down airport halls
like two drunks afraid to land.
   He's a tall, big-hearted man.
At Christmas he dressed me in Irish green
pajamas, roomy enough for his large hands to fish
me out, to find my moister parts.
   The closer we get, the harder it is
to live apart. I have to picture his bristle mouth
on my petal lips, sense where hands have been,
dream us to bed where we love
in shades of Valentine pinks and reds.
   And how does white lace figure in?
It's thinking life could ever be without him.

Tortoise

Months ago my daughter and her man made love
on a sandy beach, lay in water clear as their life's path
coming in breaths shallow as the sun-drenched time
that beat on their lone backs
together.
       Now, the tortoise, his work done, swims away.
In a ritual old as time, he leaves for work each day,
and there she lies beached, her thinning shell of apartment wall
      readies the cradle,
        waits for the birth,
calls the old sea mare
for comfort and advice.
Lonely, she opens up her turtle eye
looking for the right spot one shoreline up
to lay this ripe egg, her job just begun.

The Watch

Early morning watch
and I'm planted on the schoolyard tarp
the white stems of my legs rooted in soil-black
hose, head like a spring bulb nosing up through layers of
russet wool coat. My hands are gloved against the
penetrating chill.
"Even the Earth can see her own breath today," I hiss
watching other people's children tumble off
buses into the morning mist, isopods who've found
their legs, as they spill onto walkways
some in shorts, thin sweats, their brown hands-
"morenitos" they call them, blossoming
 into cheap cotton gloves.

      Where are my own kids, I sigh, the ones I watched
through days that melted into years, who left the cradle of
my arms for the geography of independent lives?
      And now more children move across the frozen
turf, chiaroscuro, dragging backpacks along with
the ripening cantaloupe sun. They crunch over a field
of frosted grass even scads of seagulls won't touch.
My nostrils thaw, enough to catch a whiff of onion-garlic-
salsa breath and somewhere
someone's cooking lunch.

      Watching, I begin to pace like a wife on a
widow's walk, eyelids up, flag for trouble, hoping kids
will call, come home to visit, praying
no one's lost at sea.

The First Time

The first time I really looked at you
you were soaking up the limelight
in our friends' kitchen, like the tin man
looking for his heart, wistful in blue water
eyes and a raspy tweed jacket.
        It was that soon,
the tintinnabulation of bells going off in my
corner of a circle of friends, my legs still slim
in sleek black slacks, a grey pearl pried loose
from the cloister of single living.
        How brave of you, even more courageous
than the cowardly lion to plunge in once again
claiming my heart as the one you were missing.
        And now the years stretch out on a bed of
intimacy rare and sweet as grapes that grew on
our ancient, gnarled vines. Old age sets up camp
right across the street, the neighbor who puts a
tin can in her microwave, ready to explode. If
that happens to me, love,
will you still know me?

The Anniversary

I never knew my husband's
only son
but I can almost feel the bullet
that killed him
the one that tore open his dad's heart
and left it bleeding, bleeding.
          My man says I'd have loved his boy
hair dark as that night on North Beach
the long slender body, left-handed
fingers like mine.
          Two shots of him sit framed
on my seldom-played, out-of-tune Steinway
stark black and white like the death of a child
leaves you, drained of all color.
          As his father slumps in a chair and sobs
on the anniversary of his only son's death,
I try to imagine the moment
the call at 2 am that murders sleep
shatters your dreams, whose ring still sounds
in my lover's head, the memory of which tonight
will sleep in our bed.

The Good Cook

(*for Mark*)

If you could see him at the market
you'd understand,
the good cook picking out the best ingredients,
baby greens like those he raises on his Fresno "farm" –
how he bypasses the whitest mushrooms
ones he taught me to scalp, hook my nail
under the lip of superiority, peel back the top
layer to get at the meat,
the heart of the matter.
        Tonight it's mushrooms of color,
pale gold or russet umbrellas that hide out
where even rain can't find them
in the deepest forest, giant Redwoods protecting
us on walks we took in Humboldt where he taught
me to be aggressive mounting steep hills
taught me to walk up hill backwards to challenge
those untried muscles:
Morels, Chanterelles tossed into the sauce
for a richer mix, his singular Bolognese:
two kinds of meat, white meat pork and beefy
red Cento tomatoes hand-crushed, a splash of
milk to disguise two pungent anchovies
and then the hand-held pulverizing blade,
the mix mash of altogether, a cultural
blend on the tongue.

My son in the kitchen last Thanksgiving,
the spigot wide-open, inhibition
flushed away by big reds
as his bigot of a father ranted his drink-fueled
rasp of insults— you'd understand
why my son announced
how happy he was I got the divorce.

Heavy Leaves

This spring the Dahlia didn't show
her indigo face, blanch and blister of
drought, the perennial bulb still down
in the rubble of a promise to flower,
roots tangled like mine
with the kids' talk of
moving away.
           Months of summer sizzle.
Swords of afternoon sunlight poked through
dining room shutters, my legs akimbo
over the arms of a lounge, its rich soil-brown leather
fertile in the hope of coming together
one more time to feast at the table
gather in gaggles of grown-up bodies
crammed into the tiny kitchen-of-the–broken-tile
sink as they chat while I cook,
their green finger vines
clung to stemmed glasses of
           Riesling, Pinot Noir
           a great Cab that will bleed
yet another year's ring of wine blood
on the family tree, the table glossy
and well-oiled as a summer tan,
walnut cracked open, we pull apart the frame
drop in two heavy leaves to stretch us
to the outer limits of dining-room space,
the chairs soaked with us, their sea green pattern
lapping up our after-dinner laughter, endless stories of
late-into-the night games of
Chinese Checkers   or
Blitz.
           Overhead, the fanlight whirrs away
anger, forgiveness for years rung out:
those who drank too much, grandkids
who squabbled over who sits where
at the table that feeds us all, that
brings us all together.

Goodbye, Santa Barbara

Goodbye
leaves me
homeless,
roaming Antique Alley,
a shop with the past for sale.
Click clack of footsteps
on a loose brick floor -
exploring Lewis and Clark
my rucksack full of us.
Burnt summer sage still
on my lips.
After La Fiesta
the sidewalk confetti swept clean.
Sparkly streamers shimmer
in the boulevard trees.
    Night shade down and every kind
of creature crawls out, dragging his own
kind of homeless.
    At the stoplight
a snapshot moment: Dressed up in his best, the
Balloon Man decorates a storefront window:
dapper in top hat dropped
down over sodden eyes,
sleeping it off with his stash:
gasbags for sale in various
delirious-
ly happy neon colors
    twisted into grotesque-
ly happy shapes.
       Danish at Andersen's.
 that last morning together.
I want to stay,
          have to get on the road,
"I love you" at the confab of our cars
slipped into my
beggar's tin cup.

At the Fish Grill

(for Patrick)

At the fish grill you nudge open a glare
of plate glass door, juggle our lunches
sink into a seat next to me, a shiver of
cool wrapping my shoulders, a sudden
breeze lifting my freshly-washed hair.

A late lunch but I'm hungry for talk as we
launch into saucy loud-mouthed tacos, the
fish coming on too strong for me.
The light finds your eyes, closes down your
pupils to pin points, those wide dark pools
I'd hoped to dive into taken over by stun gun
bright mesmerizing aqua, like the Venetian
glass lamps I lost in the divorce.

How I wanted you untouched by that blaze
the other me who tried on sexy outfits
at the Back Street Boutique, a sip of Sherry
to loosen inhibitions as I planned to make
another kid with your dad, the snake charmer
as he took me at the church retreat, the two of
us slipped into that god-awful trailer bed,
making it in God's-green field planting
a fifth pea, you.

"Can't you do something?" wailed his mother
when she heard there'd be another, and
then his vine got snipped, but not before you. How
I rocked and rocked us through labor the night you
were born, the bentwood chair yielding to the
weight of us, my rainbow tent dress bursting at the seams
as I waited 'til the last minute
hanging onto you as long as I could
before letting you go.

Sleepless

After counting numerous wood slats
on two walls of windows and finding them
all there, I left the cradle of our bed, padding
barefoot over four oak wood floors,
pushing through three fir doors
to slip under one very heavy down blanket
on my old, single life bed, and there I lay,
like a guest in my own home, an ocean of
house between me and my snoring husband.

    The antique French "lit," suitable for
one, rocked me gently on the edge of sleep
as cars blew their horns into endless night
and sirens on their way to a fire wailed
their wakefulness.

    Finally, the half of me still there
dozed off.

A Reckoning

(for Jack)

It's been three years since she died,
the day she walked out into "The Light"
leaving all who loved her in the
dark of *why*.
   At first there were words of condolence,
emails to wick away the pain. Then the short notes
stretched their legs to become letters: no ink, paper
or stamp, only a flick of the finger and they flew
over the continent between us. Old acquaintances,
now friends, finishing the *same* book at the *same*
time, often watching the *same* old movie.
   It was January when our words became flesh,
a birding trip out West, lunch with the Pi Phi
sisters, you and your son, Jeff, joining us for
dessert, my golden apple crisp, a taste of me. Will
he know me without the red hair bled brown from
chemo, and the glasses?
   Backlit in beach light you sat across from me, a wry
smile that turned girl gab intellectual. Not a crumb of
time left, I tucked under your wing for a hug, a good-bye
peck on the cheek, and then the two of you
flew away.

Separation

(for Tony)

When I heard you'd moved out
I already knew, every day walking my dogs past
a neighbor's sick house, the walls a jaundiced pall
of empty. Even the half dead California Pepper,
breathless in a chokehold of vines cried, "Leave" –
nothing left here except one lone lamp flickering
like a dying heart.
    I watch you now as the whites of your eyes harden
in determination, their yolk centers still runny with
emotion as you tinker with our broken furnace, you
who could always fix everything
but this.

The Moons of My Eyes

(for Ace)

The moons of my eyes have entered a new phase:
two thirds water, aglitter all day watching our sweet
sick dog stagger through his lost dream of pounce-
play, chasing a bird, or joining in a bark fest with the
pit bulls next door.

His eyes lock on Dad's favorite chair, morning
go-to place with its field of tapestry flowers, the
cushion a ledge too high, too steep a mountain to
climb, he finds he can't take off with ragdoll legs
from a wood floor
slick as ice.

Afternoons, I find him washed up on the shore of
our sea-blue sofa, unable to leap up, and now I think
how desperately hope needs legs to fly! Even the
priest pulls the cowl over his head, bald of excuses
as to why the innocent must suffer, why the most
vulnerable have to endure the indignity
of slow
          leak
                  death.

Franklin Delano Huxtable

The dark spot on his leg bone
was like a shadow on
the sun, a light we naively thought
would never go out.
       The limp,
            the yelp of fear
that fateful night,
how he hated thunderstorms,
a look of dismay percolating behind
the soulful fire in his amber eyes.
   Our gift to him was a splendid yard
with hills to climb, those herculean legs
that flew across the lawn in figure 8's
zigzagging back and forth,
old, but still a pup.
Louisiana Catahoula Leopard
dog of the spring-loaded feet, the boy
who could jump the moon at mealtime
for kibble or a hardboiled egg.
Bouncing brindle-furred skin, tough yet
sensitive enough to absorb my husband's most
soul-etched sorrow.
A nudge of wet nose under the obliging hand,
Hux, the hound dog was always hungry
for "pets".
       "Bodhisattva Dog," my man says,
Teacher of us. Enlightened.
The December night we lost him,
we lost Christmas.

Seconds

(for Lee)

It's not the years
it's the seconds
like the fifteen that leveled
Santa Cruz,
            San Francisco,
                        Mexico City
the split second it took a vein to burst
in my friend's brain, leveling her and all
who love her. It's the one that shattered
our president's brain, plunging a whole nation
into chaos.
            Lives that turn on a dime
like the time I sauntered down the airport ramp
to visit my second husband, in his city
for the first time, his beaming face
my only moon that night, this girl's eyes fixated on
his perfectly-airbrushed, silver fox hair.
I wasn't even nervous as we wheeled through pitch darkness,
snaked over hairpin mountain curves in his classic white Caddy.
 "Hope you like my little house," he cooed, knowing
we'd live there together some day, and it took
mere seconds for me to slip out of my old clothes
into that new life.

Saturday Morning

You knew me that Saturday morning
in bed, the day I ached with desire
to sleep in, your fingers prying open
the oyster, probing my parched folds
dried up as old headline news screaming,
"Leave Me Alone!"
I'd had it with work that week. Oh, how
I wanted to sleep late, but you
had other ideas remembering
how much I loved to make love
early in the morning,
loved to wake up to hands that kept
moving up and down my thighs
and then I'm wet like the Times caught
under a sprinkler head, soggy
yellowing in streetlight long before dogs'
jaws wrap around old rubber-banded papers
and aging toes find their slippers
find my thighs to tinker
with, retrieving my sex drive
and then we were making love
and I was suddenly soaked with desire
coming so high into the morning
light, relishing how you remembered
my desire to do it with you
when we were just waking up.

Mine

Last year when my Lily cat died
her warm body sagged onto my lap
like an ermine muff, my hands searching for warmth,
for life, in vain trying to hang onto her.
How I struggled
to keep the river of her crystal blue eyes
from flowing into that black sea of
nothingness.
For four years she was all mine
and then she left without my permission
like you leave each day going down
into that colliery, descending with each puff,
the stark blue of your eyes like a miner's light
that leads the way
down into the dusky shaft of cigarette smoke
dragging you, down,
                    down,
                              down,
chipping away, clogging veins
then up to the surface
coated with grit.
        I hover at the pithead, tremble with the rest
of the mothers, listen for the siren
praying you'll rise out of the shaft, be on the lift
so I can wash you back to life, the pitch of your body
clean and pure again like the first time I held
you in my arms, unstained.
        My Lily never did grow bigger,
a heart stunted like yours is going to be
from nicotine
but I know you can't help it 'cause
it's in your blood,
it's in your blood.

Marriage is Such Simple Pleasure

Marriage is such simple pleasure
days we just hang out together doing ordinary things
like the dragonflies that flit, skimming over the
green lake water.
Then times we get naked, end of our pier
swan-diving down to the murky bottom
mired there in the muck of disagreement
but rising to clean air.
    When I awake each morning, sodden with sleep
I want you beside me like two continents rolled apart, come
back together, married land masses reconnected.
Why, whole peoples have walked over
land bridges like that back
in time
        when man and woman really needed each other
        when they had not evolved to separate
        when living was in dying for one's mate.

Lily Poem

(August 22, 2004)

Light cradled in my arms as death lifted her away.
Frantically we searched for a Sunday vet, fire truck
to douse the blaze of fear incinerating our hearts.
Holding her while my husband sprinted for help,
I sank like a stone on the concrete step.
Fragile as dandelion fuzz, my girl drifted away, eyes
turning black to see in the darkness of leaving.
Emergency door locked, no answer, there was no one
to buzz for help.
When we finally found the white cross, it was
"Too late, sorry, dear,"
the nurse whispered as I surrendered my babe, limp as
a torn bean bag losing its sand.
        Head unscrewing itself from my body, I spun around
to see a woman with a sick black tom in her comforting
arms. My husband's hand shook to fill out the papers,
too late to ask for another cat life.
She had flown, that joy we had known
for too short a time.

Leftovers

Thanksgiving over,
the carcass picked clean.
Our house is quiet after the storm.
My kids and theirs have all gone home
so I walk up Carol St.
wind raising issues with the trees, tearing off
reluctant leaves, their soft shoe
dance down the street,
and out of town.
Last night's rain was no more than
a hiccup,
today's sun flirting with
leftover clouds.
Along a block wall gray as death
shoulder-high roses bend low but don't break
blooms that escaped the cutter's blade, their necks
weighted down with honey milk.
One savaged blossom lies face down in the dirt,
unashamed at being left to die.
I lift, shake the water sparkles from its hair
and head for home
feeling, I don't know why,
empty
after being so full.

Langosta

Night in Baja comes on faster than his five o'clock shadow.
Salting his Corona, my husband squeezes limón into his brew
and we were off again, kids in tow, pulling three tons of trailer
with a Chevy Suburban, an iron snail
dragging its home.

The road snakes through hills, warm and inviting, dangerous
as we plunge into the dusky shadows of twilight. The Mexican Gulf
glows pewter and purple late in the day as we push on.

"Can't stop now, gotta make it to Loreto for langosta, lobster snapping
fresh, muy sabrosa, drenched in butter," he chants, cerveza being
no more than a teaser.

"It's time to stop!" I groan, "Getting dark, there's open grazing
making it difficult to see around every corner of my worried
mind," I warn, my teeth grinding into my bottom lip as the wheels
hum on and he guzzles his beer.

In the back seat our babes babble on, oblivious and then I see it,
or is it *three* cows drawn to a late-in-the-day slaughter and I know
they might not make it across the road. Suddenly we are braking,
braking as slow motion terror takes over, and the last cow doesn't make it.
Smash! the windshield fills with cow face terror, her eyes frozen in death
and now I'm eating my heart in chunks, definitely not the lobster,
I never planned on steak tartar under shattered glass,
my arm oozing onto the carpet and then we are spinning
out, careening down a six-foot embankment
to root at the bottom of a gully.

The kids' shrieks tear through the hills!

"Mom is bleeding, she's hurt, my window smashed, and a scary man
is bleating out sounds so foreign, Spanish? Then one of the boys offers,
"Dad, the man just wants you to help him get the cow off the road!"

After three tries we are back up on the road, creeping into town.

At dinner, no one speaks a word.
Dad orders langosta, and
no one orders steak.

Lake Michigan Sunset

(for Chris H.)

I sit on the edge of Michigan
last night of vacation melting into my drink.
It's been years since I've seen this sunset
drag its bloodstones across a late dreaming sky.
My name-sake nephew with red hair,
fireball fuzz of youth, takes my hand as we unspool
into his fishing boat, buzz-saw across the lake
then chug into a little cove to anchor on the cane back
shore foamy with snails, our heads fast-dancing
through gnats, clamor with mud-mucked feet over
mellowing sand dunes, rise, then sink out of sight
as we dip in and out of mild inlet water,
Appaloosa-wild in the dream
that summer could last.

The sky hangs onto day, still pink
saying nothing, our feet planted like ancient
pilings that jut ghostly heads from Michigan's
chill lake. I pick up one fossilized stone heart to
skip over lapping water.

Daughter-in-law

(for Leslie)

I know you.
When I die you'll be there
to bury me, or sprinkle
my gray ash like rose petals
over the marriage bed.
I know your fragrance
like the pungent Plumeria branch
that quickly took root
in my backyard.

    You and I have that rare commodity
beyond texting and telephones –
real time together, and when your
sage green eyes well up, their water
will always mingle with mine.

    Tangled in a bracken or deep
in forest shade, somehow the light
always seems to find you.
When you said "Yes" to my son –
"Yes" to the chiseled jaw and
thin-lipped smile, I knew you
would follow me anywhere,
that my people would be
your people, my God
your God.

Jenny

You were blueberry pie, a seasonal treat
coming in summer.
　　　White gauze gown hiked above ample hips, I lie listening
to his morning snores thrum like insects in thick green grass,
remembering, thinking of 'three little boys and no girl'
that churned envy in me each time I heard someone had one.
"It's probably another boy, about seven pounds," the doctor needled
teasing that pricked me right through to where your ripe melon
body shifted, the promise of pink flesh under the white cheesy
newborn coat, the slippery seeds my seed.
　　　How quiet you became those last weeks, calm in the storm
of disappointment, with me finally believing that a male tumor
had eaten anything pink.
　　　By August skeins of hope no one could unravel,
the rosy girl's hat I'd knit that would stay mine like childhood
summer days at the lake, bare feet dangling off the pier, submerged
in cool lime water that swallowed my calves,
white as fish bellies.
　　　The day you were born I was ready: perfect like all those
Swedish pancake breakfasts, sausage curls in place, a flutter of
false eyelashes, make-up with iridescent powder, and glowing.
There I lay, stretched out, calm at last, awaiting your debut, no
pain too great.
　　　You are blond perfection, Lake Michigan sunsets at
the Big Beach, stellar blue eyes. The bedroom fan whirs overhead.
I lie awake dreaming as your grandmother waits by the phone, washing
blueberries for an August pie.

Images of Us

The old Caddie humming by farm fields
humps of fertile earth, wet as our love.
Over the flat road we rolled, through
Watsonville past other lives, a
church where once you married
someone else.
          Stopped down on a park bench,
we sampled Carne asada, tamales, the sun
at Gizdich Farms, fresh ollalaberry pie
tender slice of life as you asked for my
once-married hand.
          My berry-stained lips sighed,
"Yes, of course I'll marry you," but then you
knew what that raspberry mouth would answer
pouting for pictures we took to prove
we were living the dream.
          Down the mountain we headed for home,
wound through a thicket of fur-brown hills, their
rumps wall-papered in ring-gold leaves.
"Did that day really happen?" I gasped as I reached
into the empty cave of my camera to find the film
had unspooled itself, memories of the day you
exposed me to the light again.

Granddaughter at Fifteen

(for Cat)

Granddaughter at fifteen is a colony breaking
away from the mother country
firing her cannon blasts on cyberspace
raging to live on her feet rather than die
on the knees of parental submission.
      Wanting to be part of the game, I cross over
the line to watch as she charges down the court, a
blue blur of sidelong scowls dribbling past, no care or
recognition that I'm even there.
      The storm warnings have always been
in snapshots: a sulky look only the royals can master,
a deep-throated chortle at six months
when she discovered spaghetti.
      Born on Father's Day, subjects queued up
waiting at the stage door as she tunneled down that
royal red viscera, cord-strangled, a cyanotic
bundle of blue squall.
      After,
as water broke calm enough to drink in the
amazement of her, a tiny sprawl of new "Cat"
on her grandmother's lap, I guessed her fifteen
would be like no other.

Free

(for Rachel)

My granddaughter loves all things free:
foot-loose days in France, a rented house
in Alsace, the tall windows flung wide to
exhale onto lush vine fields.
   She revels in doors open to the flies,
their crazed kitchen buzz, backyard cherries
ripe for the picking and keys that escaped with
the last renter, returned to unlatch the mysterious.
Rachel insists that Nazi spirits still rule
in the dank, musty corners of a cellar
where non-Aryan socks disappear.
Even her teeth are free, newly-unbraced, flashing
happily as they sink their wide pearly arch
into croissant délicieux.
     At sixteen, fresh from her childhood chrysalis
she perches on my bed, resolute as a stalking cat, teetering
on the edge of all her tomorrows with my camera poised
for the perfect shot of a *moth* trapped behind
a net of bellying gauze curtain.
     "No, *butterfly!*" I insist,
bedazzled by the amber-laced blur, and then the whirring wings
rest. Stopped down there, she sits with grown up patience waiting
for one precise click just before the after when we open the window
to freedom. For me, nothing can trip the shutter
of that moment.

For Christmas

For Christmas they bring five pairs of azure eyes
deep as Crater Lake or pale, shallow pools
fringed by desert storms, the older sons' locks
darkening like a late winter afternoon.
    Slowly, I sip the draft of holiday time
when my children swim back to me.
Feast over, extra table leaves torn down,
the succulent ribs stripped clean, eggnog froth
the only thing left in a giant bowl redolent of
our own sweet mead.
    And when the last child has gone
I mourn, covering mirrors like a Hebrew
Death of time used up, no graven images here
only their eyes and how I looked in them.

Far from My Tree

These days
the apples fall far from my tree,
their young, green skin ripened red
in a fever of divorce.   Sinewy, nimble of limb
pith for the clutch and climb,
for reaching up to patches of steely blue
where the sky's the limit.
        They've left the tree
left it to night creatures that scrabble across
the roof of my mind, keeping me awake:
furry, bush-tailed or bandit-eyed
rabble that rob sleep.
    I must trim the branches,
stop milking dead days of every last drop,
curtail critters looking for shorn clumps
of tousled heads, pairs of agate eyes,
or fiery blue gone cold.
    Somehow the bandaged knee never quite heals,
those babes in the night
crying for ma-MA.

Emma Waits

for the boys
who tickle her tummy
the ones who allow her to slather them
with kisses,
my boys who have grown up and gone their own way
who now have sons of their own.
She sits resolute, erect on her dais of kitchen floor
a bristle of ginger fur standing at attention,
the white ruff puffed out, eyes deep furrows of
thought.
She listens for wheels up the drive,
the needle nose on point toward the glossy
sun-dried tomato door
flung wide.
   Light dances across the slick red door
and my furry girl knows someone is coming
'cause I've baked two quiche pies instead of one
unearthed the chest of Rose Point silver
spread the table with meringue-white linen.
Even the wine goblets are singing
in anticipation.
   Shadows all tucked in for the night, outside the
moon is a sliver of pearl nail breaking through a
deepening sky.
   Trust is in the air. Miss Perez is walking
her dog "off leash," and *anything* is possible.

Shibui

(For Mitsi)

The rose blush valentine waits to be discovered,
open on my son's desk, his romantic scrawl a
sign of marriage
to come?
   I could only guess about her: half
Japanese, the sweep of sleek raven hair
western or almond eyes? I had never
met   Shibui,
the single Japanese flower:
its stem her slender crisscrossed legs,
full-lipped concern, one elbow crooked
the cream-cupped chin at rest in her
delicate porcelain hand. Wide-set eyes
riveted in deep conversation with my
husband, her body the lone bloom on
the bamboo rim of the
cistern of water.
               Born in 1940, I understood
that the war was finally over, her pregnant
shell of expectant body, my granddaughter
a blend, and then, when she was heavy with
their son, how selflessly she nursed our
friend on his last day: pristine sheets, pillows
propped, the final meds before he left; how
neatly she swept up the mess of dying.
By then I understood shibui's quiet strength,
this daughter-in-law of mine.

Catherine's Birth

Family gather outside, hover at the labor
room curtain, like a stage door, waiting for you
to emerge to thunderous applause.
Each wave of pain brings you closer
pulses that carry you
to a shore called life.
Catherine, already royal in blood necklaces
the blue head turning scarlet with lusty cries
open eyes, as we, your fans, fill you
with our held breath
let go.
       Strong character,
we pull the message from the green glass bottle
of your mother's body. Father holds you up to take
a bow, pink as a kitten's ears, he rocks you in his
new-daddy arms, checks the parts, stories from
the players who came before, wonders how we will
fill you up.

Breakfast for One

My daughter-in-law always skips breakfast.
Too much salt on her tongue for a healthy marriage
and now my son stands to separate
the fragile egg poised over a cerulean bowl
as he cracks,
breaks it, the edges too jagged
too uneven a break
to fit back together.
                    Now comes the drool of disbelief
while he coaxes the opaque slime
from its yolk center
nudges it from the gleaming circle of life
its fertile red "eye" still intact,
a rich gold world of second chances,
only part he'll eat.

Baby Wait

My daughter sits
rock resolute, a boulder on her lap
under a crust of taut skin that waits
to shed its dark secret.
Soon her breasts will be snow-capped
food for the child who will mount its assault toward life
plate tectonics, move her legs apart, thunder its head
down the path to light.
As with every major quake
we will be moved,
we will be changed forever.

Santa Cruz

He's my sweet, meat-lovin' man
rare mind with tender parts, a reader
of books, a domesticated 'cat'
who wanted me at home with him,
the one who swept me off my feet
in the Fells' kitchen that October
whisked me loose and reeling
past neat rows of Castroville green,
their once-crowned artichoke queen
a young Marilyn Monroe.
He showed me another way to get stinkin'
wheelin' us through wafts of Gilroy garlic
over flatland sloughs peppered with
salt-white, long-plumed egrets,
to land on his quaint 1924
bungalow steps.
    Sometimes, I'm still there, like we never left:
together at Shoppers Corner, the Buttery
slicing and dicing, baking my apple pies in
that two-range kitchen, tucking potatoes into
their cool, dark bin with Hux curled up on his
"good dog" bed, so happy my man once cooed,
"Ever get up to Santa Cruz?"

Ace Man Cometh

We met on-line, fell in love, really
so blown away was I with
the tumbleweed hair
a medley
   of soot and ash
          and earthen brown.
A long hair, my kind of
'man' even though too young, I feared, to leave
his mother, the redhead Gwen Verdon.
But then there we were driving home
no words needed, just the touch and taste of
his long tongue, licks to each salty curve of
finger burrowing in to find his too large
rib cage, big enough
for both our hearts.

   Seven now, his dog time ticks faster than mine
soaks up sun, sprawled out on the furry green
his hair now mounds of frothy white and copper red.
Just like the male animal he is,
he notices every thing about me: a stalker of
my tennis shoes, signs of when it's time for a walk.
And his demand for on-time meals,
the chocolate eyes melting me
into sweet subservience.

   Oh, when our beloved hound dog died,
when Christmas was eclipsed by his cancer
when finally the mourning fog had lifted,
then did my Ace Man cometh.

3: WHAT'S IN IT FOR ME?

What's in it for me?

I ask
feet jogging in place
work-weary-save-my-spot-while-I-check
airplane status
tripping over less than an hour to
flight time
roped off
juggling carry on bags
in a circus rush hour LAX
waiting in skin-soft-as-he's-ever-touched
under an intense green dress
nipped to a 24" waist
just the way he likes it
beading up under Perrrrrrry Ellis
alpaca much too much fashion coat
I will never need in Texas
waiting to buy the ticket
while the wait grows obese
one man screaming obscenities at the ticket agent
who says the ticket's no good
for tonight?

What's in it for me?
I ask
a go-stand-by desk upstairs
past security
past clicking cream-colored Bally heels
echoing past trysts down an overlong
tundra of airport
agent double-oh-no-you-can't-go tonight
who says "maybe" with prevaricating lips
and I wonder how to call you in Texas
from a credit card long distance
select your service phone
you call my home   hang up

not there
as usual I'm taking too long to come
while you wait for a plane to drop me like stolen luggage.

What's in it for me?
I ask
retracting-once-more-into-worn-out belly
landing gear
groaning metal bird feet tucked under
spitting fiery protests
at being overloaded
flying me
picking over wilted snack salad
one cherry tomato
no dressing
wine stolen from first class
ninth class hotel room waiting for me
after final drag around semi-destination
airport
sleep wound around my passion feet
walking   walking
officials dragging port for
my dead body
with a message
from you
two black men shaking heads over 2 a.m.
brooms find me
the drive to Ramada Inn West
stuft into an airless room
phone call
you on the other end getting
closer   closer
your sleepy voice
waking up lie of Rio Grande
musty water sweet voice
hair unrumpled after three wispy hours
of no sleep sleep.

What's in it for *you*?
you ask with a
filibuster of hands
cupping two breasts
spilled out of cups
the intense green dress torn off
whole day city behind blackout curtains
you pull shut   from choice
our choice time together caught by the throat
catching on your belt buckle
undoing me
in it,   with you.

This January,

only one week of grace,
like some unopened Christmas gift
found.
And now the relentless rain
in a clime unaccustomed to gloom.
At first stutter, drops,
then full-blown sheets of it
to sweep the street.
Next a persistent drip, drop of
determined, enough to carve
great gouges in stone.
    Today coming down a steep grade
the fog is so thick I can't see
any life but my own
tucked into that hillside,
and beyond, the unknown
a falling off into uncertainty.
    I know there will be leftovers
scraps to toss or deal with,
all the dross from a winter storm,
and the clearing away of
trampled blooms.

The Little Fisherman

The cur of constant controversy
barks at the heels of
the little fisherman
peeling off the last line
of reasonable thought
undressed
by the hollow chatter
of a canting fool.

Dog Walk

We brave torn streets,
Jackhammers pummeling
cement curbs into chunks,
rearranging the corners of
our lives, pipes new
arteries to carry the blood-
water to our thirsty bodies
and dying lawns.
　They are building soft-
studded corners for the
disabled, *viejos* who stay
breathing longer now.
　A democratic defecator,
my dog pushes out her pre-
poop at the blue house, then
moves her bowels to the red
one down the street, fresh
fertilizer, if I never picked
it up.
　Sharp blades whir and slash
to bring errant plants to heel,
cut and shape, hatless *campesinos*
straining in relentless sun, their
mowers daily background music.
Star Jasmine and Rose mingle with
the smell of man-sweat as we turn
onto Ryan, wind up Circle Drive as
one hundred years rattle by over
rubble, a Model-T out for a Saturday
spin as we trundle over broken cement
blocks, past orange cones that warn
of John Deere Cats snoozing in the
sun up ahead; my well-oiled arms
begin to sizzle.

As my dog and I head for home
a Latino couple is on the move,
la esposa twelve steps behind with
pink plastic lunch pail dangling, his
recycled bicycle loaded with tools
for car-washing, peddlers at twenty-
five *dólares* a clip.

Swan Song

I came often, in-
between wives 2 and 3
crept over his hair-mossed heart
lodged under shoulder blades
that cut water,
rowed for Harvard.

Tall
Tender-is-the-Night
doctor who examined my long monogamous
swan's neck, deciding I had been
a swan
too long

and leading me slow-dripping
into the Velvet Turtle
cushy-chaired afternoons
we'd lunch
drink rare wines
turn off
the Tuesday beeper.

Black hair
balled shiny, one spot where
my nude self shone brightly
I have napkins sprinkled
with Goethe poems
drawers full of musty wine corks
an iron box jammed with
steamy, shriveled, scribbled
cried-on letters
pictures of his four sons
an only daughter who still clings
and chills my cream neck, this child

his nuts cracked open by loving
me.
I think often of our
last time together
my birthday.
His candle burned and dripped
all afternoon
copy of Playboy open
to playmate of the month
double-truck breasts splayed
brushing the Gideon Bible
a half-eaten submarine sandwich
premature ejaculating wine
trying to breathe.
And my gift
a Nikon FM2
so I, slow to develop
would keep discovering
him, frame by frame.

Rain

Finally, two weeks of rain
ends and still its babble,
murmur of kids' voices below my window
whoosh of cars on the highway.
Morning squeezes juicy and warm
through my blinds, slices of orange
on a butter yellow wall.
In canyons beyond my cement garden
mud rules, rearranging lives
people's houses.
Hope is underwater, all mucked up
the way you left mine
the morning you said
we're done.

Queenie at the Queen's Hotel

At last
someone who needs her
to bare something besides teats
to squallering pups
he calls her by a
lover's whistle, bitchtail flying
she knocks things over so eager
to get there, bird-dogging
the freeways
she arrives at the Queen's Hotel
loose hearts flopping under raspberry
silk she looks sheeny in black linen
pants greet everything about her
friendly, he feeds her too much 'water'
as they trade stories of a
dog's life, he the master
his tongue hung out
asks if she will love him
after chowing down
she heels to the penthouse
strips to the bare-bark-belly
under all that fur
they fall across the bed
balling, animal and
trainer after
the choice milk running
from her mouth
there's a drool on the pillow –
woman, man's best
friend.

Monkey on My Back

As a Merry Prankster living in Zayante he kept
seven Monkeys, yes, seven in a man-sized cage
where they could swing from prehensile tails, hands
free to offer, plead, argue each case before a sympathetic
jury of conscience.
Seven monkeys locked up tight, he'd feed them
perfectly good waste, produce scavenged from alley raids
on super market dumpsters.
"Seven?" I stammered, as his seventh wife
feeling the connection.
"How does one acquire that many monkeys?"
          and then he spilled,
"Once one person gives you a monkey everyone wants you to
take them off their hands," and soon he had taken them all, or
so it seemed, he continued. "Monkeys want out, want to spread
their mischief, but only the Macaque, the Alpha monkey,
gained freedom at times, the one who stared back
with primordial recognition."
          I pass by the "safe," the too-hard-to-crack roll-top desk,
its thick cubby hole doors locked, the key squirreled away
in a drawer somewhere, well-hidden from me.
          I stare at the monkey in the mirror, trying to figure her out
preen hair to stay clean, still wishing
they could come out to play.

Lunch Break

All lunch break long
I stood....
watching clouds break
watching planes break
through clouds,
      land,
me face up,
      looking,   waiting.....

They laugh at me
the clouds with their control
have me,
they with their control of rain.

Tears soak, tear me through
out of control,
watching for you   watching
the way you used to watch
planes   take   off
break through clouds
          land,
before you knew me
when rain had nothing to do
with
us.

Lost Jewels

Die, Daddy, and take the one bright jewel
a sense of who I am
in your pale skin.
Mother lives in Aunt Kate's locket
shy child's face
snapped
shut.
I am open
to the pearl skin
looking for the gold stick pin
to close my dress.

Misplaced the ring of happy
early marriage
cabochon hump
of innocence.
I keep the jewel box open
invite theft, taking out a long string of Tuesday afternoons
spent with a lover
knotted in-between with talk of marriage
leaving his second wife,
my dumbstruck husband who filches and sells my
earrings screwed into gold post holes
and how we bled and bled for love
and I am still not healed.

Mother says, "That's alright, the children are your jewels,
wear them," but they are leaving one by
one day she decides I really am her daughter, gives me
the jade necklace you gave her,
takes it back saying she can't remember
giving you away,
Daddy, you are so far
and eternity's the ring missing five
stones and I am blitzed
in his leather-buttoned car
making it without glitz, Daddy,
only the unzipped
family jewels.

Infertile Woman Syntax

A period begins
the sentence
fresh-caught men-
strual flow on an always
white gauze
pad.

She had hoped
this month
a baby
for punctuation
to start the line
her age being a factor
in miasmal disappointment
rising like the yeasty smells of
warm monthly blood.

She knows Depression
in her thirties
raises one yuppie husband
a career, two bone-tall dogs
so easy to walk at night
the unborn babies sleeping between
her well-exercised legs
she shakes them loose
one ripe fruit falling
its split skin yielding seed
black clot, one black dot
to end the sentence.

I'm Having a Divorce

twelve years gestation
the judge cuts into
my belly full
C-sectioning
pulls
dark things to light
after months of feeding information
to attorneys who nurse things along
make all necessary changes
they ask about reconciliation
I say "No" more fat complacency
burn the fat lady's clothes
fatter I got the hotter he was
with new positions for
sticking it in.
Blonde children was all
I ever gave him
now dark is coming to light
through a black hole fully dilated
pains getting closer together
son 22 plans to marry
in summer, my perspiration beads
the bride's dress, I see her
piquant body in labor
want to calm her fears with
years of marriage anesthesia
play dumb, go numb around the edges
as attorneys arrive with
bags full of string for untying,
tying the newly pulsating cord
I'm cut loose, won't someone please
boil some water,
spread the papers for signing?

Feast of Steven

Properly baited,
I swim through the city
up Canal, past Erie
to West Huron
wishing to leave the fish school
of shadows following light
the taxi stops at your boat
bobbing in blue surge
fix of eyes
you fish me out, all smiles,
the feather-lipped lure shaved off
my fisherman
as you reel us through
a spinning door
guide my killer-sharkskin dress
mother of black pearl shoes
we sit, fin-mouths flopping
we eat Italian with our hands
fasting now and then, adjusting
the lines, eat pasta slipped between
sips of champagne
a celebration, lips moving through a dance
of bubbles rising in our glass throats breaking
in delight to find me untangled
undressed on your plate.
    Still alive, I release my clammed-up sand
my tail foot finding your male feet
play, our waiter offers to cook me up for you
strongly suggests more liquid
I'm beginning to smell
should be eaten soon
or thrown back
fish out of water, feasting, choking on air,
wishing you didn't have to
throw me back.

Death Notice

Feeling a strong need to connect on line, instead
I find you dead, your friends writing worthy epitaphs,
"Gangly charisma,"
"Too young to die."
My hand trembles on the keypad, the bold black letters
blurred around the edges.

      Outside, a harvest moon warps misty to the memory
of your long fingers tracing my neck and shoulders,
a hotel room made beautiful by the glow of two
bodies wrapped, smiling, unhurried,
in the discovery of touch.

      Above the obituary the words, "Join Face Book for a
chat..." Macabre, how one is invited to talk to the dead, the crisp
white-shirted arms that encircled me as we kissed,
wine-soaked lunches beneath an adolescent tree
that had to grow older to say good-bye,
so we could finish other lives we had started.

      I draw a hot bath, raise the window sash a
crack to let steam escape. It's Saturday night and a
blues tune floats up from the restless boulevard.

You would have liked that.

Chill January

you left me
a thick new skin
slogging home
after work
the blue crush bus stop
fat grapes pressed into
stained seats, stench of
6 o'clock bodies, woozy breath
sun's firewater rising in window glass.
I burn down with all the rest
strain to hang on
through one more lurched corner.

We wedge in
cram for a chance to sit
throbbing feet after long-standing
the bus slimmed in a final purge
of exhausted flesh.
Stop like a wheeze bag death rattle
the doors squeegee open as I slip out,
swim into the dark-water night.

Lights stammer on, a lit fishbowl.
I can't see them but they're watching me
reach for home, not home with you, my kids gone.
The guard dog moon flashes its cold eye
you still behind every turned key
breathing in every unmasked corner
fluttering our bed sheets
what was and is our flame
gasping for air.

Casa Malibu

My shoes cast off, falling off
to non-
    cha—
       lance.

High, heeled over
Sleeping it off in a corner of Casa Malibu,

veranda'd

shoes waking up to watch you
slip me bare
arms, round tumblers
locking into place
fingers unzipping my body

stockings, hipsters now
    cornsilk dropped off
    milky-threaded thighs
    sweet silk yards of
    pin-loosed hair.

Barcas lurch on hooks
to see you up to the gunwales
in
me.

Sea birds circle camp,
starflighters to shoot the waves
salute our "baby" cries
beached,
    husky
       whispers.

Battle for the Bed

I fight for sheet supremacy
but you have a chokehold on my portion
of the covers.
My weary body has been relegated to
the trenches, the outer-most border of our bed.
I dangle near the edge while you take
yet another hill of mattress.
So jealous am I that you sleep
and I don't.
And now the latest in weaponry,
a wind tunnel of stale exhaled breath
blows across the virgin plain of my clutching arm,
whipping up a whole field of hairs I never knew I
had, all the breathed-in moments of your spent day
blown out, second hand life shared in such
an aggressive way.
Still I lie like one dead, casualty of war, not moving
a muscle for I remember last night, how hard
you fought for sleep
while *I* slept,
and it's okay, darling,
I'll stand watch tonight.

4: LATE IN THE DAY

We Visit

hospital, great aunt
strapped in her wheelchair
ready for flight.

Little sparrow
with feathers for hair
chatters and chatters
we sandwich her in
between grocery shopping
the car wash
crumbs of our time
to keep her going
feed the convalescent bird
money going at two thousand per.
One makes reservations
for a death like this.

Blue veins under
tissue paper skin
blood under layers of
bed sheet ice, the bed waits
to freeze little sparrow
in death tucked neatly
with hospital corners.
We turn to leave
toss one last morsel
we'll be back on Friday,
we who are too busy living
can she remember?
If meals-on-wheels doesn't need us,
if our homework is done.

Sleep

Sleep has left my bed
moved on to a younger woman who can
handle it.
The storm-blue walls close ranks, agree to keep
slow-wave slumber from washing over me.
Hope dissolves under my tongue as
the cherry white wafer seeps in, rough-edged
crystals like crackle glass.
I lower my lids, REMs searching
wide awake.
    The windows are tight-lipped, white haired old ladies,
sounds and smells of the day locked in.
Garlic hangs around in the stuffy, soporific air.
    My clammy feet and hands thrash
the weary sheet into a torqued shroud.
I am dead-tired
and sleep like a reluctant lover
who refuses to come.

Princess

Look,
a true princess is born
to know pee
from love stains on the royal
mattress. She needs a
bladder tuck and while
the plastic man's at it why not
liposuck, fill, make bigger
breast sacks made empty
by mothering
and lift those hooded eyes
giving her the look of eternal
surprise, remove the ugly lines
from a face that once looked
like a young Princess Grace.
    In surgery the doc lays back
the top layer of skin
face meets heart, sutured just
below the hairline, healing skin
so itchy, so numb she's afraid
to go out in the sun
or have friends meet the new
her, bored that all the king's horses
and sharp-knifed men can't make
princess happy or satisfied that
the bladder pees less often
the breasts don't sway naturally
or feel right beneath his fingertips
hers painted blare-red once a week
holes filled every other and when they make
love, careful not to scratch too deep.

Russian Dolls

Black clouds hold their tears the way
I hold mine. I think of you, Mother, in hospital
that expensive holding tank for old fish who
forget their lines, who wait to swim
back to God.
    My daughter's hair lies like manger grass
across her swollen belly. We clasp hands over
the new heart growing there, reach in with murmuring
voices, whisper plans for the opening.
    And you at the closing.
I imagine you dressed for the occasion: wood-proud as a
lacquered Russian doll that opens to smaller ones inside,
you who opened to me, and I to my only girl who now
awaits the birth of another.
    I think of you, Mother, in hospital.
Before you moved, we could still share: squat down to chat
in PJs on your living room floor, look at old pictures, tape
stories of your growing up that spliced us together, and the
taut telephone lines, how they kept us high-wired across
silent chasms of space.
    The lines pulled us through, Mom, the way you pulled me
through chicken pox, the mumps at fifteen, through my whole
young life and now the lines are down. I can't touch the old
heart dying there, can't bring down the fever
of hovering death.

Phoenician

(for John)

When my brother and I were kids
I'd often lay siege to
the attic door, his third floor fortress
a Forbidden City
where he'd spin dreams one
black platter at a time,
playing d.j.

I'm back home from the colonies
of marriage and divorce.
Now we wage war
same side of the door,
our mother caught in the net
of old age.
We take life one island at a time
anchoring the little Sunfish
when lake winds get too wild.
My big brother, the cautious Phoenician
at the helm. He steps into the swirling lake
repositions our sail as we ride this out together.

Late in the Day at Agave Park

The mango sun is going down like a bitter pill.
I follow my shadow uphill
slip into a close of ink-green pines,
scent of slow escape filling my nose as I teeter over
a ridge of uprooted cement, my feet negotiating sharp crags
crackling over empty husks and pods.
The retired tennis court lies littered with nettles,
the once-solid slab floor a map broken into new
countries that bask in scrolls of late afternoon sun.
The net is despondent, no more Love played here,
its ruched old skin sagging between two rusted iron poles.
A squirrel scrabbles up a tall pine that's losing its hair
one point at a time.
Languid swings hang lifeless, no throb or pulse now, their
laps fallow and forgotten.
        I think how peaceful to be centered down
on this solitary splintered bench, watching the warp
in moss-drenched calm, the only war here being
the one we all lose.

Indian Summer

Trees surrender
their reluctant leaves to
Indian Summer, laying down arms,
curled and withered, the rich crimson
and gold bleeding out to a parched brittle
chestnut. A brisk fall wind rounds up stragglers
on the road to the chamber, a pile for heaping on
and then the burn, the acrid smoke
a holocaust with no survivors.

Cocoon

My mother becomes
her mother
in a cocoon of late life
feet out of circulation
swollen piano legs cut short
at the ankles by lace up old lady shoes.
Beethoven's deaf is marching.
I feel the vibrations of last moments as we
search for words with no small meanings
    Such a loss; maybe my final visit
and already she's laid out on her chair in front of
the TV, robe-swaddled in a chrysalis
of becoming.
    Midnight and I feel her eyes
at the foot of my bed, amber orbs blazing
through darkness, the desperation of
a wounded animal watching
me sleep.
She covers me with worry,
begs me to help her remember
her morning meds.
        Mother has chosen Monday's child
to do the laundry for her, shampoo, lather up her hair,
still streaked with the smoldering black of youth.
Day, and we brave the market where we parse prices
bicker about everything including too costly Granny
Smith apples for a peace pie I want to bake.
        Back at her apartment
thank God you call, ask if we can meet as she demurs
and I make my excuses, bundle up against the chill
catch my breath on ribald humor you're thrilled
I get. Santas on street corners ring their bells for me.
All the old men want some.

Blood Draw

Withered by sultry heat, I cool off to wait for
the butterfly needle, blood drawn that might
reveal how soon my story will end.
  She sits across from me in a wheelchair, her daughter
perhaps, nattering on about someone's wedding as the
enigmatic smile finds me, slowly ripples across the white
glass face, still smooth as sweet memory milk. Thoughts float
into that other life, lips like ripe fig skin slowly splitting into
some kind of recognition.
  I feel I know the eyes, the face that holds them.
We were neighbors years ago, her two eyes like pitch coals that
flared as we played watchful mother, raised a cluster of kids our
youngest, Pat and Mike, pals on the dusty dung trails around Laguna
Lake Park where they scavenged, fished, spent twig twirling days
together, children we raised safe as the golden eagles that nested
high atop our towering eucalyptus, survivors on Clarion Road
circling driveways like horseshoes clanged together
at the stake.
  How quickly we burned through a decade, Ash Wednesday's
smudge that won't wash off wrinkled foreheads, and now a nurse calls
the name I couldn't remember, "Laverne Francis," and the daughter
turned mother wheels her past my hesitation to speak, into the belly of
the medical office, and whoosh! she's gone like a wisp of smoke,
without a word.

Bath

I took my bath the
way he took me
slow-drawn
                    and
                            hot
my blood stirred, skin raw-rubbed
by his bristle hairs, submerged
to the eyeballs, free-floating
like the fake dead, then shooting up
for air before drowning.

Now
I marinate in tubs of
what ails, deboned, half-eaten breast meat
islands, their jelly-blob nips
that bleed like late night eyes.

Face it
No one juices to lukewarm
leftovers
brackish water, smells of
growing mold
things that clog. Even my bits and pieces
won't wash at the drain.

Antique Drawer

I crack the antique dresser drawer, teasing inch by inch, coaxing it to release its
matchless scent. Like a reluctant lover, it opens to me as I hook my fingers through
ormolu pulls, laurelled wreaths that once graced victorious heads. It groans like a ferry
easing past the pilings. Eagerly, I hang over the brittle box breathing deeply of its
contents. The warped wood is a blend of aromas: snipped Havanas, newsprint at a kiosk,
Sumatran beans, oily and black as jet. From one corner, a red scarf screams for attention.
She scrapes her silk skin on the timeworn, splintery wood. Amazing, how this drawer
holds history together without a single nail, its rabbet joints still a tight fit, the recalcitrant
smell seeping through the pungence of powdered lining, past two centuries to the time of
Louis XIV. Here also are the artifacts from my transitional days like a bracelet with
charms, black with tarnish. It smudges, pricks my finger as I fumble through time. While I trace
the outer patina of wood, I dream back to my Uncle Jim in his jaunty hat. He has
driven my grandmother and me to Holland, Michigan, 1945, and it's Tulip Time, flowers
rioting outside our cabin door. I can feel my child's feet hit the floor, race, bounce across
the drafty wood, a blend of warm and cool.
Suddenly, I hear bare feet padding up the stairs. I can taste the brass key, acrid
and metallic, as it twists to seal the past. Like the ritual after lovemaking, I wash up, hide
the twisted bit of brass. My granddaughter is coming and she likes to explore old,
unlocked things, like Gram's chest of drawers.

Nineteen Rings

1.

The ancient continents of our bodies shift
in the water blue bed. New landforms, crusty
skin-tag islands in an ever-rising sea. A climate
change so hard to navigate at times like the day
your tall tree of a body toppled over, flailing and
crumpled on our bedroom floor as an ambulance
wailed its siren symphony
up the street.

2.

Nineteen new rings, circles on the pine trunk packed
with years of us, a Christmas tree sprig that outgrew its
tinseled pot. Now the tree stands like a sentinel on the
terraced hill where one rain-drenched March, years ago
it lost its grip on mud that slammed through the
fence built to keep our dogs at bay.

3.

On one high branch, a majestic hawk pummels his prey,
fragile and small as our days. I think his plumage, how
deep the color like new soil, and the appetites of wild
birds, a flurry of grey-haired feathers fluttering down.

Catch and Release

My child is 'father to the man'
the dad who until now thought
we didn't need a fifth, this son
who ignites the flickering fire,
kick starts his dad's dead motor
in sad winter, tirelessly cleans up
the mess when he unloads.
How ironic! The boy who hated
to read books is finishing the
story I began.

When our marriage flagged, he asked if
the child really was *his,* so unlike in looks
but then their love of fishing, how both throw
out that catchy line, set the hook, how easily
they release anything too small to eat, the dad
who used to keep a stringer full of girl-fish
until he decided I was
a keeper.

The caretaker dreams of escape, slips away
at dawn, his Evinrude set on soft purr, the boat
a silver arrow that pierces still water. He knows
bass hug the shore, finds a snug cove, the lake
smell pungent with possibility like the dream he
never quite lands: his move to Wisconsin, a fish story
that grows bigger each day, the one he has to throw
back for now.

The Exam

Slacks and shirt peeled off, casually draped over
the cold stone bench, rumpled elephant-gray skins
laid out empty of me, my shoes footloose, poised
on the barren floor, ready to go it alone, their
laces far flung, loose as my thoughts that float
back to how it used to be when I wore young,
firm flesh.

I hang out naked in the exam room, waiting for
the doctor to arrive. He calls for someone to
witness his touch, before he pokes, prods my
layers, the still velvet, intact walls of my vagina.
He tells me everything feels fine: the dark channel
that gave my babes their path to first light,
first breath, he assures me things will stay
moist, wet as fresh paint
with that hormone cream.

I beg for a refill!

Humped over in the chill, my backbone curves into a
question mark under the baby blue drape, open down
to the crack, he chats on about his latest grandchild, a
need for a 3-dimensional mammo of
my breasts, the dried-up milk sacks that
nursed five kids so long ago.

I dress fast, knot my Nikes
for the run home.

Jeanie

Hey, walkin' girl, we've come far since Midwest
winters. Did we trudge through the same snow piled up
on brick-limned North Shore streets, plunge laughing
into the wet sop, walk to school when the freeze
seals your lids, and buses quit?

Two women who now care for two brothers,
men who made us sisters. Sis, I wish I'd known
you then. Did you brush by me, saddle shoes cruising
down polished school floors? Or were the two of us
a tableau in summer stretched out like fresh bait on a
sweltering beach, our well-basted bods smelling of
orange Tangee or coconut oil, shading eyes as we
checked out the cute guys?

We grew up to leave The City, board the El to town.
The Loop that goes round and round, wheels that
clattered over steel rails as we left Linden St.,
rattled past the fatal third rail that killed Richie's
curious brother, his mother's grief that screamed
someone could die here!

We kept going, past the endless mouse-grey back porches
of the affordable, down into the screaming tube, into the
dark dazzle of other lives only to return to what we once knew
what we didn't know we loved
until now.

5: POLITICS FOR LUNCH

The Flag

What has happened to our flag
the symbol that once hung proudly in
World War II windows, draped caskets of the
dead, so sacred it must never be
dragged on the ground
or burned ?
    On July 4th, a sacrilege as
fireworks rain down on our
wood shingle roof.
The neighborhood houses wince, littered with
American flags no bigger than snot rags, each one
branded with "Made in China" and a realtor's card.
Day after the celebration, I find one face down
on the sodden lawn, my neighbor's flag
strangled by its own pole,
    And then the incredible news story:
a Pit Bull immolation, the sad dog trussed up
with fireworks and set ablaze by someone who
thought they should get him first
before *he* got them.
Did they savor the stench of burned flesh,
the singe of his sleek, smoke-grey hair
his shrieks of protest, the fact that
he survived anyway in the loving arms of
a shelter volunteer? Wouldn't the amber salve
of euthanasia be better?
    I take down our American Made flag
big enough to cover us all, rolled up to
stow away in the hall closet.
    In the wake of celebration I unfurl my red white and
blue veined legs on a patio chaise, lounge in the solace
of sun and silence, my freshly-washed nightgown,
blue as shallow water, waving on the line. The wind has
cut in and they dance on without me.

Soap Opera

Somewhere inside my aging mother
deep as winter her frozen edges begin to melt,
too dangerous to chance in spring
and now she wants to go there
cling to the ancient pilings of her lounge chair
as the t.v. console flicks on, a new chapter each day.
The Hero, one who saves lives, crosses a continent of
rustic cabin floor, handsome in summer skin with
burnt-toast lashes, he opens up to touch.
My mother flutters like a stunned bird's heart
as he navigates daggers of splintered wood
whorls of sage eyes deeper than mermaid
the heroine's reed-slender body wrapped in
ruched, kendal green dress.
He offers her an orange like a whole world
on fire in his encircling hand. She reaches
back, slowly cupping over his fingers
hers pale as a white sand beach, hands knotted
together in the ecstasy of touch.

Sinkhole

The earth opens its jaws
wide, a sinkhole swallowing the young man
whole, voracious maw that drinks cars and
people, water that meets *karst,* the chalky
layer of crumbles that can't hold
up a house.
    At first a slow seeping in, then the slick
acrid odor of survival, rumble of hunger
caving in on itself, an entire life choking off
all sound
to dead silence.
    Poor young sap,
once a student-of-the-month, buried alive
sucked away in his sleep, his version of
the good life an oubliette
of credit card debt.
    His stunned brother crosses the tape,
digs in up to his elbows, searching for his
kid brother who thought he'd ride it out
underwater, skim the surface 'til next pay day,
snorkeling along in that torture chamber
of delusional
forgetting.

Politics for Lunch

Girl friend to the far right of me twists her napkin
in anguished disgust, sandwiched between
two lefties as the political rhetoric spills over
like boiled milk.
The server lights our candle, arrives with tea party
and lemon, the main dish smothered in debt reduction sauce
spreading over all three plates, sanguinary viscosity
a black-scarlet like dried blood on the battle-weary wounded.
A boundary line traced with a well-manicured finger,
we raise right hands in pledged resignation, swear never
to discuss politics at lunch, *that is* off the menu.
With lipstick fresh as war paint, we pay the bi-partisan bill
slip past tables, chatter, tinkling like broken glass
stand in wait at the little girls' room,
"Now please don't talk about me!" she begs as the
door sighs shut and we hope the flushing toilet will
drown out our whispers.

Malaysia Flight 17

Beleaguered airline.
Summer of the missing,
298 souls unaware they were over a war zone
as reluctantly they lay down their arms
and legs, a pelting of body pieces,
char everywhere.
Thirty-three thousand feet above Ukraine
80 of them children going home
or on vacation high, but not high enough
to escape the deadly missile, the bloated body
pieces curled and wilting
in a blister of July sun.

    And now the drunken soldiers scrape up
all the minced flesh on the road to the
cooling chamber, all the pointing fingers
and toes packed in for the first leg
of the final journey home, and then
the weeping.

    Who did this? Who's to blame for such
atrocity, a game the dead can't play, or
can they? One intact carcass tightly strapped
to its seat, cradled in a pale salve of wheat field,
one crooked leg with its knee crossed over an
indicting arm with one finger still attached,
points East toward Russia.

Shopping in the Year of Corona

The bodies pile up in the
make-shift morgue. The
dead call out to us,
"Use our blood to smear
on doorposts, so the virus
can pass over your house."

I gather my shop bags.
We need weeks of food to fatten the
victims. Hollowed out by worry, I bump
and groan over potholes, screech around
corners to get to Sprouts. Tight-lipped
clouds say nothing while I search for
a parking slot at the Farmers Market.
Before "social distancing," the frantic
crowd swoops down like a swarm of
locusts, buzz-sawing through whole crops:
corn, wheat, flour, fruit and eggs, anything
greed can grab, not one herbed-chicken-to-go
left in the coop, many of the shelves'
slicked bare.

She rounds the corner in Vitamins,
my daughter's friend no longer an imp
at her fourth birthday party, she calls me
by my first marriage, the eyes once
burning suns eclipsed by fear, she
needs a hug more than bread, says she
shops for her mom, 93, now
sequestered at home.
We tap elbows instead.

Time to queue up, five check-out lines
snaking all the way back to produce.
A lady begs me to keep her spot as
she leaves to scoop up the leftovers
in bulk food bins.

Outside, the rain tries to wash away the frenzy.
I need to cover my sad face, baby blues peeking
over the horizon of a flimsy paper mask, like a
thief getting away with the goods.

Influenza

> I had a little bird called " enza."
> I opened the window and
>   In-flu-enza.   - a child's ditty

1918: She sees him through the gauze of delirium.
A fever dream, her dashing young lieutenant has left

the trenches, gone over the hill into a No Man's Land of
the sick to fight for her. Handsome in silhouette, he

pours water from a wavery glass, soldier lover who
loosed her laces, slips the drenched body into an

envelope of ice white muslin. She knows his touch,
the soothing fingers that try to massage the raging fever

down from her head, fire that has moved up the lighted
torch of her slender body, the abundant chestnut hair

blanched white, then falling out.

He is her pole-star, a fire never slaked from the beginning,
night of their first carriage ride, an echo of horse hoofs on

the cold stone street, hot steam rising off wet flanks. His
touch so subtle, erotic, the tick of rickety wheels

rocking them together, their shoulders cobbled as he lays
his bare hand over her gloved one, teases the pearl clasp

open, he unsheathes her fingers one...by.....one, their naked
hands laced together; she feels only one pulse,
one heart beat.

Katherine Anne Porter, journalist, writer of short stories, is left to die in an obscure hallway, but she lives! She has defied the odds, the obituary filed away for another day. But, alas, her young lieutenant is dead, his life for hers, victim of the Spanish Flu.

"His death has divided my life in two!" declares Miss Porter, a love story that never grew old.

.

Lemons

The gardener tells me to pick them.
Juice and freeze the lemons, put the empty
shells to rest so that the young buds can
flourish, but I want them to hang there
a while longer, time to sweeten the sour,
let them bask in the shade
of gloss green leaves.

Then a slip of the moon behind clouds,
a mask for roof rats that climb to high hanging
fruit, peel off the face so the mouth can't talk,
their zest dangling ribbons of flesh stripped down
to the cheesy white pith that dries in summer air,
like Deng's dogs hanging from
Lima's lamp posts.

I walk off my anger, past houses grander than mine,
olive trees so ancient time has forgiven their scars,
the twisted limbs declared magnificent, branches
that reach out to me, still living despite
a life of bitter fruit.

The keening wind slipstreams me into a private
park. An interloper, I drop the weight of my years
onto a child's swing, blue-veined legs like the map
of where I've been. They pump me higher, so high
I may never want to come down.

6: A CANCER

A Cancer

The climate is changing.
The lilac bush blooms all year round,
now on the parched branches of my arms,
skin deep lavender bruises rising daily or
raspberry clusters, tiny blood islands
floating in my cream skin
close but never touching.
As fingers rake through loose clumps
of golden hair once thick with envy,
I pluck, throw loose strands to the birds
to silken their nests.

Lawns get along on two days water.
Hundred degrees blisters our driveway at 3 pm.
We burn through the rainless winter nights
when my bald head, slick as an egg shell,
can't sleep.

If I feel a chill or fever coming on,
the nurse warns to call 911. The clanging fire
truck clatters down our street twice a week
rescuing an elderly couple surviving old age
one more day, one more night
in their own home, determined to leave it
feet first.

Lost

Impossible, yet another four hour drip
drug infusion, my body laid out on a stretcher of
lounge chair, head tilted back on my own feather
nest of a pillow. Above the bald capped orb, a
tangle of clear plastic tubes docked at my chest port,
a virtual army of chemical warfare going in like
troops charging off a Higgins ramp
wading through the roiling waves of my blood
to hit the beach for all out attack.
"May I offer a cozy warm shroud to cover?"
she mews, "Now relax, think of something sweet."
                On the beach at sundown
years ago, the buoyancy of salt water
bobbing heads of my children at play their faces
chiaroscuro at dusk, backlit, indistinguishable
a catch in my throat as the wind gobbled up
my warning screams, their shadowed bodies tossing
in the surf.
        That was the day I lost time
as it unbuckled itself from my frantically waving wrist
dropped down onto billions of spent grains of sand
centuries of hour glass run out under my feet,
my ingot watch, its pure gold face flush down
in the water.
            A whole night under relentless tidewater
stripping all hope of recovery, time piece
a precious gift from my husband, lost forever.
And then the next morning, as determination prodded
my sandy feet, trying to retrace washed away steps
I found it, what were the odds, the slim band raising
its skinny arm like a stick of driftwood or a crab's leg
lost no more, time reclaimed, my part of it
given back.

Wigless at the "Y"

I opt not to wear a wig
and now my baseball-capped head
makes me anonymous in this expanse of pool.
My friend, the Boston-born blonde, squints
at me across four months
of my chemo aerobics:
tortoise shell glasses instead of contacts
lash-less lids, eyebrows that need to be painted on,
and now my legs float out
from under me.
    She swims closer like someone who's glad
she isn't Chris: the pal who needs the red flag
of recognition, my copper hair
burnt out, gone
along with ten pounds
six chemo workouts,
months of shots and scans
countless blood draws that drained away
all that ginger,
my signature look.
    After our professions of love and concern
have echoed through the salvaged ship,
we hug, the ocean between us crossed.

Hair Loss

My hair is giving up, tiny fingers hanging
from the precipice of swollen follicles
letting go
capitulating, chemical warfare too much
like mustard gas in the trenches,
R-CHOP chop, the bodies cascading
down the curved hillocks of my shoulders,
whispering across my back to lie dead
on the marble beachhead of my bathroom sink.
Strewn now with the dead, some afloat in the small
pond of my half-filled sink, or sunk to the bottom
like shimmering copper pennies in a fountain of hope.
How gloriously they used to close ranks over my ears
my lost troop of tresses burnt out. How they'd march
across the back of my alabaster head to protect or
pouf out in sartorial splendor atop my cream crown
in strands of late summer sun,
gold or sienna like burnt toast.
        Now I gather up their lifeless bodies
like fallen leaves dropped down in clumps
or alone, lying strewn across my counter top
some in gentle s-curves afloat
giving out with moans and whispers,
some clung to the slick drain
not ready for a trip out to sea.
How I mourn my lost hair!

The Messenger

(for Andy)

After weeks of treatment:
chemo that made you crusty, son, radiation
drying up all that good juicy mucosa,
it was all out war with you off to battle each day
wearing the same fatigues.
I needed to hear the healing sound
of your voice
to know if you'd been able to float up
through the turgid green waters of pain
toward the light
and, after all, it was your birthday.
But when I called, the cell phone warden
snarled, "That message box is full."
Then the barking outside,
an animal ruckus as I cradled the phone, chill
with disappointment.
When I wedged open two thicknesses of door
the dogs bubbled past me like uncorked champagne
and then I saw him, a tiny bird stopped down
on the tarmac of our patio, flight delayed,
last remnants of a six-day rain pooled beneath
his spindly feet on the pewter gray cement.
His eyes were glazed over in stun-gun stare
and I was sure he wouldn't make it,
his mussed brunette feathers, pink poked flesh,
dog bites perhaps?
        "We have to do something!" I moaned, as my
husband eased his large hand into a plastic bag
and gently lifted him onto the launch pad
of the hot tub.
"Maybe the steam beneath the lid will revive him
and he'll take flight," I hoped as I slunk back inside
swabbing down wet dog drippings on the wood floor.

And then, with one swivel of my head
he was gone.
      I imagined the moment:
Piper Bird lifting off
Lucky Lindy, tipping his wounded wing,
barely making it over the soggy pine boughs.
I could picture his mother somewhere nestled
deep in the branches, hope sounding from her tiny
beak, "Come on, son, you can make it!"

The Light

1.

He was an accident of birth
a pea dropped into my pod
to plant there for a time, steely
vine growing strong enough to truss up
my heart as he fought his way out
toward the light.
And now he shows me
how to fight against a dark enemy
Cancer, a legion of one
my doctor son
on the phone
talking my fever
down, building a moat -
fortress of two
mother and son
in a conspiracy
of one.

2.

Church doors padlocked against the night.
Portals that were always open
keep the faithful in,
the doubters out,
the ones who *need* that light streaming
through a kaleidoscope of stained Irish
glass windows, their timeless story:
Jesus, the Jew skewered there
our Lord wearing his crown of thorns,
the dying head lolled to one side,
arms arched, pointing up
like a lighted menorah.
And the two Marys in their blue glass
robes splayed at His feet, His side
pouring blood,
his pierce-ed side.

3.

Oh, the clear red trickle of love
so pure
you could drink it.
        But night has drunk the day
snuffed out all the living light,
saint window sentinels along the walls
slunk away in darkness
and now I am sick, feeling alone
with my feeble faith in doubt
and I pray no one asks
me where I think
I'm going next.

Love Child,

Let's bridle the horses, clear the saddlebags
of all "devices,"canter over to that clump of
trees by the river, our legs sprawled or curled
like contented snakes in the sun, fishing lines
thrown out, sinkers adjusted, waiting, waiting.....
eyes to meet or not and talk, like we do at times
about important
things in life.
    Do you remember that tiny kitchen in France:
the aroma of dark roast, buttery croissants
from Barr, yogurt diaphanous as chiffon. And
Mark baking his homegrown cherry tarts?
If it hadn't been for you two I never would have
gone, jetting over the Pole pretending I had no fear,
claustrophobic, wearing your decompression hose.
You saved me as we travelled to France for
two glorious weeks I will never forget.
    And when the sinkers dove to the bottom,
a really big fish on the line, after you insisted
I get that 'Catfish scan' – discovery, Lymphoma!
You were there bringing it up from the bottom,
fighting with me all the way.
    The day you were born, when Dr. Singer held up
your swaddled newborn body and you looked me
in my exhausted eyes, when he asked
"Where's the Dad, why isn't he here?" I knew
it'd be you and I against the world.

Monarch Butterfly Sanctuary at Santa Cruz

They've come so far – flown on fragile wings
the great migration across thousands of miles
to rendezvous in Santa Cruz.

Three generations whose fourth will live
longer because of such a reach to find
the perfect milkweed place
to lay down future eggs.

In the Sanctuary of Monarch Butterflies
I sink to the grove floor, thrust living fingers
deep into the trampled mat of fallen leaves,
offer a prayer, thanks for the wet
promise of life.

November chill and the sorrel wings dangle
in their blue gum Juliet sleep
wait for warmth, for 55 degrees or more
when they will soar into

the dappled light. We wait for the communal sigh
when a million wings lift off in red-gold glory
high as the gift of time that's been
given to some,

but not everyone.

We form a circle of remembrance
for Margaret, a young woman I'd never met
whose friends have gathered to paint living stories
of a vibrant girl who, like Icarus, flew too close to
the sun, who bravely tried to defy

the Father's will
be done.

We clasp hands, send her up through the colossal trees
on a quiver of butterfly wings.

Chinese Soup

(for Andy)

Ever since you called to tell us
about your cancer, I can't seem to
get it right, clouds piling up
like dirty laundry I never get to.
That night
my husband was making gallons of Chinese soup,
enough for all the victims,
the delicate, gelatinous bodies of rice noodles dancing
in the hot chicken broth, grazed by bits of
Chinese sausage in the big swim, and then
the phone rang, you spitting out
the bad news
cancer, squamous cell carcinoma of the tonsils
that swam down the river channel of your neck
blood to form a new land mass.
With rhythmic grunts your news gobbled up
all our appetite for soup,
the volume turned down low, flame whisper
of hope sounding
and all I could hear was the silent thud
of disbelief
as Chinese herbs and spices simmered away, the
looping rice noodles breaking up into tiny pieces
while they melted into one impenetrable mass.
It was then we decided to pour it all down the drain
since no one was hungry anyway.
   Outside, elephant-grey clouds trumpet, gather on
the plain of expectant sky, their fog edges feeding off
the tops of trees.
And then the pounding rain begins.

Close

(for Ace)

I wear his eyes,
char brown kukui nut lei of
eyes that encircle my neck, their candle
oil still burning long after
      I watched them close
      for the last time.

When Summer turns blue,
I wear his fur to ward off the chill of loss,
walk the hills clothed in his sun-red hair
shades of copper-gold and cream
      Welsh Corgi ruff.

I keep him close,
new pup keeping up as we trot out past old haunts
like the sun-blackened wood fence he never could see
through, never did discover who barked to him from
the other side.

I burn through Summer in my mourning garb,
to Fall when I must open the gate at last
and let him run free, the way he never could
that last painful year.

About the Author

Christine Quarnström, a Chicago native, likes to say she wrote "Goodbye" in the January snow and headed for Los Angeles. That was when she transferred from Purdue University to USC where she earned her teaching degree, settled down to raise a family of five, and then teach middle school for almost twenty years. Chris sings in a Whittier-based master chorale, Chorale Bel Canto. Retired now, she lives in La Habra, California, with her second husband, journalist/writer, Lee Quarnström, and their adored Welsh corgi, Rose.

Acknowledgements

I want to thank all who have encouraged me in pursuit of my art, poetry: the late Stephen Levine, Buddhist/poet; Austin Straus, poet-teacher; Jeanie Elliott, Janet Albaugh, Sister Margaret Barrett, my children and my husband, Lee, whose unfailing support and encouragement are endless.

Thank you, also, to Linda Langton, publisher, for helping to make this creative endeavor a reality.